LONGMAN

CORNERSTONE

A

Practice Book

Anna Uhl Chamot

Jim Cummins

Sharroky Hollie

PEARSON
Longman

Longman Cornerstone A
Practice Book

Copyright © by Pearson Education, Inc.

Pearson Education, 10 Bank Street, White Plains, NY 10606

Staff credits: The people who made up the *Longman Cornerstone* team, representing editorial, production, design, manufacturing, and marketing, are John Ade, Rhea Banker, Liz Barker, Kenna Bourke, Jeffrey Buckner, Brandon Carda, Daniel Comstock, Martina Deignan, Gina DiLillo, Nancy Flaggman, Cate Foley, Patrice Fraccio, Tracy Grenier, Zach Halper, Henry Hild, Sarah Hughes, Karen Kawaguchi, Lucille Kennedy, Ed Lamprich, Jamie Lawrence, Niki Lee, Christopher Leonowicz, Tara Maceyak, Katrinka Moore, Linda Moser, Liza Pleva, Edie Pullman, Monica Rodriguez, Tara Rose, Tania Saiz-Sousa, Chris Siley, Heather St. Clair, Loretta Steeves, and Andrew Vaccaro.
Text composition: The Quarasan Group, Inc.

ISBN-13: 978-0-13-235695-4
ISBN-10: 0-13-235695-3

PEARSON LONGMAN ON THE **WEB**

Pearsonlongman.com offers online resources for teachers and students. Access our Companion Websites, our online catalog, and our local offices around the world.

Visit us at **www.pearsonlongman.com**.

Printed in the United States of America
9 10—VOLL—13 12 11 10

CONTENTS

CONTENTS

UNIT 4

UNIT 5

UNIT 6

Name _____ Date _____

Vocabulary

Use with Student Book pages 8–9.

Key Words

neat

city

luck

flower

mail

A. Choose the word that *best* completes each sentence. Write the word.

1. With a little _____,
   I will win the race!

2. I picked a _____ from
   the garden.

3. The mail carrier brings the _____.

4. Many people live and work in the _____.

5. Sam's new bike is so _____.

B. Unscramble the words.

6. a l m i _____

7. k u l c _____

8. y i t c _____

9. w o r f e l _____

10. e t n a _____

3

C. **Answer the questions.**

11. What things come in the **mail**?

_____

12. Where do you plant a **flower**?

_____

13. What place do you think is **neat**?

_____

14. What can you see in a **city**?

_____

15. What brings you good **luck**?

_____

Academic Words

D. **Read each sentence. Write a new sentence using the underlined word.**

16. We go to school in our <u>community</u>.

_____

17. My <u>role</u> in school is to be a student.

_____

 **Take a walk in your neighborhood with a family member. Talk about what you see. Use the key words.**

Name _____ Date _____

Reader's Companion

Use with Student Book pages 10–13.

Cool Hector

Hector skips along the street.
He thinks, "This city is SO neat!"
To lots of people on his way,
He says, "¡Hola! How's your day?"

When Hector walks right by the park,
a big, black dog begins to bark.
Hector sees a disk fly by.
He catches it on his first try.

Use What You Know

List three people you know in your neighborhood.

1. _____

2. _____

3. _____

Reading Strategy

Tell one thing you know about Hector. Underline the clue that shows this.

_____

Genre

Many poems have words that rhyme, like *street* and *neat*. Circle two other pairs of words that rhyme.

Use the Strategy

Do you think Hector likes living in his city? Explain why or why not.

_____

_____

_____

Retell It!

Retell this passage as if you are Hector. Tell a friend what you did.

_____

_____

_____

_____

Reader's Response

Pretend you are in Hector's city. What would you like to do?

_____

_____

_____

Retell the passage to a family member.

Name _____ Date _____

Phonics: Short Vowels

Use with Student Book page 14.

> A word may have a short vowel when it has a consonant-vowel-consonant pattern.
>
> c a t
> C V C

A. Fill in the blank with a vowel to make a CVC word. Some examples have more than one choice.

1. v _____ n   **4.** h _____ t

2. y _____ t   **5.** c _____ t

3. l _____ p   **6.** d _____ p

B. Circle the CVC words with a short vowel.

7. I ran all the way home.

8. We had fun at the park.

9. Please let me stay up late.

10. The baby can sit up.

Home-School Connection List two more CVC words with each vowel. Read your words to a family member.

Comprehension: Character

Use with Student Book pages 16–17.

Read the passage. Look for clues that tell you about the character. Answer the questions.

Joy's Job

Joy has a job. She takes her neighbor's dog for a walk. She walks the dog each afternoon when she comes home from school. She takes the dog to the park. Then she brings the dog home. She gives it food and water.

1. List three things that Joy does on her job.

_____

_____

_____

2. Which sentence *best* describes what Joy is like? Circle the letter of the correct answer.

   a. Joy is a good student.
   b. Joy is good at her job.
   c. Joy is a friendly person.
   d. Joy likes to go to the park.

 **Pick a character in a book or TV show. Tell a family member what the character is like.**

Name _____   Date _____

Grammar: Nouns

Use with Student Book page 18.

> **Nouns** are words that name people, places, and things.

A. Read each sentence. Circle the nouns.

1. Sam hits the ball.

2. The children go to the park.

3. Many people work in our community.

4. The city has tall buildings.

B. Use each noun in a sentence.

5. store

_____

6. girl

_____

7. lunch

_____

**Find a sign in your neighborhood. Look for nouns.
Read them to a family member.**

9

Spelling: CVC Words

Use with Student Book page 19.

A. Fill in the blank with *a, e, i, o,* or *u*.

1. m _____ n   m _____ n

2. c _____ p   c _____ p   c _____ p

3. d _____ g   d _____ g   d _____ g

B. Fill in the blank with a consonant. The examples have many choices.

4. _____ o g   _____ o g

5. r u _____   r u _____

 Write three sentences using CVC words.

_____

_____

_____

Home-School Connection Write one CVC word with each vowel. Read your words to a family member.

Name _____ Date _____

Vocabulary

Use with Student Book pages 20–21.

Key Words

dessert

friend

fold

mix

A. Choose the word that *best* completes each sentence. Write the word.

1. I like to eat cake

for _____ .

2. I will _____ milk and eggs in a bowl.

3. My best _____ Rosa will be at my party.

4. I can _____ my clothes and put them away.

B. Circle the key words in the Word Search.

F	R	I	E	N	D	T
X	K	O	I	N	E	D
C	Q	A	W	X	S	M
R	F	N	I	A	S	E
W	O	M	T	K	E	U
C	L	E	L	Z	R	R
D	D	Y	Z	E	T	F

C. Answer the questions.

5. What do you **mix** together to make a salad?

_____

6. Why do people **fold** their clothes?

_____

7. What is your favorite **dessert**?

_____

8. How do you make a **friend**?

_____

Academic Words

D. **Read each sentence. Write a new sentence using the underlined word.**

9. I <u>create</u> paper birds.

_____

10. Making paper birds is part of Japan's <u>culture</u>.

_____

 Use each key word in a sentence. Read your sentences to a family member.

Name _____ Date _____

Reader's Companion

Use with Student Book pages 22–27.

Making Friends

Hana just came to this school. She is from Japan. Hana does not have a friend yet.

Carlos just came here. He is from Mexico. Carlos does not have a friend yet.

Miss Jones tells Carlos to sit by Hana. She asks Hana to teach a fun thing to Carlos. Hana says she can make paper animals. Her mother showed her how. Carlos thinks that is a fun thing to do.

Use What You Know

List the names of three of your friends.

1. _____

2. _____

3. _____

Reading Strategy

What do you think Hana will teach to Carlos? Underline the clue that tells this.

Comprehension Check

Why don't Hana and Carlos have friends? Circle the sentences that tell why.

Use the Strategy

List two events that happen in the passage. Put them in the right order.

_____

_____

_____

Retell It!

Retell this passage. Pretend you are Hana. Tell a parent about what happened at school.

_____

_____

_____

_____

_____

Reader's Response

What fun thing can you teach to a friend?

_____

_____

_____

Name _____ Date _____

Phonics: Long Vowels with Silent e

Use with Student Book page 28.

**Choose the word that *best* completes each sentence.
Write the word.**

> The vowel is long when it is followed by a
> consonant and the letter *e*. The letter *e* is silent.

bake	hope	like	mice
same	slide	snake	ride

1. Sam and I go to the _____ school.

2. A cat will chase _____ .

3. I _____ to go down the _____ .

4. We _____ our team will win.

5. Can we _____ cookies for my birthday?

6. Mari and Rose want to _____ a horse.

7. Jake saw a _____ in the grass.

Home-School Connection List three more words with a long vowel and silent e.
Read your words to a family member.

15

Comprehension: Sequence of Events

Use with Student Book pages 30–31.

**Read the passage. Then read the list of events. Write *1, 2, 3, 4,*
and *5* to show the sequence.**

Play Ball!

Leon and Gina play with a ball in the park. Leon throws the
ball to Gina. Gina throws the ball to Leon.

Leon tries to catch the ball. He misses it. A dog runs and
picks up the ball. Gina and Leon chase the dog. But the dog
runs away with the ball!

_____ Gina and Leon chase the dog.

_____ Leon misses the ball.

_____ Gina throws the ball.

_____ Leon throws the ball.

_____ The dog picks up the ball.

 **Read the events in the right order. Make up what happens next.**
Share your idea with a family member.

Name _____   Date _____

Grammar: Proper Nouns

Use with Student Book page 32.

> **Common nouns** name any person, place, or thing.
> **Proper nouns** name a certain person, place, or thing.

A. Underline each proper noun. Circle each common noun.

1. mother   6. Mrs. Rodriguez

2. Asia   7. land

3. day   8. Sunday

4. Thanksgiving   9. holiday

5. Indian Ocean   10. ocean

B. Write a proper noun for each common noun. Proper nouns begin with a capital letter.

11. state   _____

12. month   _____

13. person   _____

14. planet   _____

15. building   _____

 **Write a common noun. Then write two proper nouns for it.
Share your nouns with a family member.**

Spelling: Proper Nouns

Use with Student Book page 33.

Fill in the blank with a proper noun.

SPELLING TIP

Remember that proper nouns begin with a capital letter.

1. My best friend is _____.

2. My teacher's name is _____.

3. The name of my school is _____.

4. This month is _____.

5. My favorite holiday is _____.

6. The state we live in is _____.

7. The country we live in is _____.

8. My favorite day of the week is _____.

 Write three sentences. Use a proper noun in each sentence.

_____

_____

_____

Home-School Connection List three proper nouns. Share your list with a family member.

Name _____ Date _____

Vocabulary

Use with Student Book pages 34–35.

Key Words

celebrate

crowd

company

weekend

gathers

A. Choose the word that *best* completes each sentence. Write the word.

1. Do you like it when _____ comes to your house?

2. The family _____ by the fire and sings.

3. Anna and Luis _____ when they make good grades.

4. There was a big _____ at the game.

5. Rosa plays with her friends on the _____.

B. Write the word that *best* matches the clue.

6. Saturday and Sunday _____

7. big group of people _____

8. comes together _____

9. do something special _____

10. friends that come over _____

19

C. **Answer the questions.**

11. Where have you seen a **crowd**?

_____

12. When do people have **company**?

_____

13. What makes you want to **celebrate**?

_____

14. Who **gathers** together on holidays?

_____

15. What do you do on the **weekend**?

_____

Academic Words

D. **Read each sentence. Write a new sentence using the underlined word.**

16. We live in the same <u>area</u> of the city.

_____

17. Our houses are <u>similar</u>. Both are big and red.

_____

 **Use the key words. Write a story about a special day. Read your story to a family member.**

Name _____ Date _____

Reader's Companion
Use with Student Book pages 36–43.

My Family

Sometimes, friends join our family celebrations. Company gathers in our yard. Neighbors, friends, and family come over. There is a big crowd.

Everyone brings something to the party. There is plenty of food. Dad cooks. Mom makes salad. We drink lemonade. We eat dessert.

We laugh and talk. We play games and have fun. You can tell that we are having a good time. I like to see everyone together.

Use What You Know

List three people in your family.

1. _____

2. _____

3. _____

Reading Strategy

List three foods your family eats on special days.

1. _____

2. _____

3. _____

Comprehension Check

Circle two things the family in the passage eats.

MARK the TEXT

21

Use the Strategy

Describe a game you play with members of your family.

_____

_____

_____

Retell It!

Pretend you were at the celebration described in the passage. Tell what happened.

_____

_____

_____

_____

_____

Reader's Response

When do you think this celebration took place? Why do you think that?

_____

_____

_____

 **Retell the passage to a family member.**

Name _____ Date _____

Phonics: The Letter Y

Use with Student Book page 44.

> At the end of a word, the **letter y** may have a long *e* or a long *i* sound. At the beginning of a word, the letter *y* acts as a consonant.

Read each word. On the lines, write whether the word uses the letter y as a long e sound or a consonant.

1. party _____

2. city _____

3. you _____

4. community _____

5. yard _____

6. yell _____

7. yet _____

8. silly _____

9. happy _____

10. yo-yo _____

List three more words with the letter *y* at the end. Then list three more words with the letter *y* at the beginning. Share your words with a family member.

23

Comprehension: Make Connections

Use with Student Book pages 46–47.

Read the passage. Then answer the questions.

Weekends at My House

Each weekend is the same. My brother and I want to sleep late. But Dad wakes us up early. He has plans. "I know you guys want to help out!" he says.

Last weekend, my brother and I helped Dad paint. Two weekends ago, we worked in the garden. What will we do this weekend? Dad says the garage looks messy. I know what we will do this weekend!

1. What do you do on the weekends?

_____

_____

2. How do you help out at home?

_____

_____

Read your answers to a family member.

Name _____ Date _____

Grammar: Plural Nouns

Use with Student Book page 48.

> To form the plural of most nouns, add -*s*. To form the
> plural of nouns ending in *s*, *ss*, *ch*, *sh*, or *x*, add -*es*.
> For nouns ending with a consonant and *y*, change the
> *y* to *i*, and add *es*.

Complete each sentence. Use the plural form of the word.

1. chore   Dad wants us to do _____ on the
weekends.

2. gift   We gave Grandmother two _____
for her birthday.

3. dish   Please wash the _____ after dinner.

4. box   We put our old toys in _____ to
give away.

5. dress   The girls made _____ for their dolls.

6. aunt   I have two _____ and two uncles.

7. cousin   I have many _____.

8. party   Do you like birthday _____?

Home-School Connection   Write three sentences. Use the plural form of three more words.
Read your sentences to a family member.

25

Spelling: Plural Nouns

Use with Student Book page 49.

Write the plural form of each word.

1. city   _____

2. party   _____

3. story   _____

4. family   _____

5. buddy   _____

6. puppy   _____

7. baby   _____

Write a story about your family. Use three plural nouns.

_____

_____

_____

_____

_____

Home-School Connection   Read your story to a family member.

26

Name _____ Date _____

Review

Use with Student Book pages 2–49.

Answer the questions after reading Unit 1. You can go back and reread to help find the answers.

1. In *Cool Hector*, how do you know that Hector is friendly?

_____

_____

2. What do you learn about Hector from these sentences? Circle the letter of the correct answer.

> Gus lets Hector close the door.
> (Hector did it once before.)

    a. This is Hector's first time on the bus.
    b. Hector works for the bus company.
    c. Hector rides the bus to school.
    d. Hector knows the bus driver.

3. In *Making Friends*, which event happens first? Circle the letter of the correct answer.

    a. Hana teaches Carlos how to make a paper crane.
    b. Miss Jones tells Carlos to sit by Hana.
    c. Carlos and Hana help make a dessert.
    d. The other girls and boys taste the dessert.

4. How do Hana and Carlos change during the story? Circle the letter of the correct answer.

   a. At first they are happy. At the end they are sad.
   b. At first they are sad. At the end they are happy.
   c. Hana learns how to make a paper crane.
   d. Carlos learns how to make a dessert.

5. In *My Family*, how does the family celebrate the grandmother's birthday?

   _____

   _____

6. Read these sentences from *My Family*.

   > Neighbors, friends, and family come over. There is a big crowd.

   What does **crowd** mean? Circle the letter of the correct answer.

   a. one person   **c.** a lot of people
   b. family   **d.** children

7. Describe one thing your family does that is similar to the family in the selection.

   _____

   _____

Tell a family member something new you learned in this unit.

Name _____ Date _____

Vocabulary

Use with Student Book pages 60–61.

neighborhood

garden

seeds

plants

A. Choose the word that *best* completes each sentence. Write the word.

1. I like _____ with red flowers.

2. Do you have a scarecrow in your _____?

3. The people in my _____ work together.

4. We covered the _____ with a little bit of dirt.

B. Read each sentence. Write TRUE or FALSE.

5. Seeds need dirt and water to grow. _____

6. Plants are living things. _____

7. A neighborhood is bigger than a city. _____

8. Beans can grow in a garden. _____

C. Answer the questions.

9. What place in your **neighborhood** do you like? Why?

_____

10. What do **plants** need to live?

_____

11. What can you find in a **garden**?

_____

12. What happens when you put **seeds** in the ground?

_____

Academic Words

D. Read each sentence. Write a new sentence using the underlined word.

13. Mistakes can <u>occur</u> when people are not careful.

_____

14. A <u>consequence</u> of studying is learning.

_____

 Write a paragraph telling what you know about how plants grow. Share your paragraph with a family member.

Name _____ Date _____

Reader's Companion

Use with Student Book pages 62–67.

Birds in the Garden

We have a garden in my neighborhood. We all take care of the flowers and vegetables. We all take care of the trees. But we have a big problem. Birds are eating the seeds! Birds are eating our plants!

My dad says we can fix this problem. We go to the Hill Street Stable. We get a lot of hay. I carry some hay. My mother carries some hay. My dad carries his tools.

Use What You Know

List three things you might find in a garden.

1. _____

2. _____

3. _____

Reading Strategy

MARK the TEXT

Underline the sentences that tell about the conflict or problem.

Comprehension Check

MARK the TEXT

What do the people take care of in the garden? Circle two things.

Use the Strategy

What is the conflict in the passage?

_____

_____

_____

Retell It!

Retell the first paragraph of the passage as if you are a bird.

_____

_____

_____

_____

Reader's Response

What would you do if it were your garden? How would you solve the problem?

_____

_____

_____

Name _____ Date _____

Phonics: Long Vowel Pairs

Use with Student Book page 68.

> The sound of long *a* can be spelled *ay* or *ai*.
> The sound of long *e* can be spelled *ee* or *ea*.
> The sound of long *i* can be spelled *ie*.

A. List the words by the long vowel sounds. Then circle the letters that make each vowel sound. The first one is done for you.

clean	cried	hay	pie	rain
seed	skies	stay	week	

Long *a* Pairs	Long *e* Pairs	Long *i* Pair
h(ay)	_____	_____
_____	_____	_____
_____	_____	_____

B. Use a vowel pair to make a word with the long vowel sound.

1. n _____ d

2. l _____

3. c l _____

4. _____ t

5. t r _____ n

6. n _____ t

Make a list of two words for each long vowel pair. Share your list with a family member.

33

Comprehension: Characters' Conflicts

Use with Student Book pages 70–71.

Read the passage. Then write what the conflict and the solution are.

A Big Mess

"Jake," said Mom. "You didn't put the lids on the trash cans."

Jake looked out the window. Trash was all over the yard. It was a mess.

"Yes, I did," he said. "I did put the lids on the trash cans. The raccoons knocked the lids off."

Mom shook her head. "I've got an idea," she said. "We'll put some big rocks on the lids. Those raccoons won't be able to move them!"

Conflict: _____

_____

_____

Solution: _____

_____

_____

 Write a sentence about how you would solve Jake's problem. Share your sentence with a family member.

Name _____ Date _____

Grammar: The Verb *Have*

Use with Student Book page 72.

Subject (one person)	Form of *have*	Subject (more than one person)	Form of *have*
I	have	We	have
You (one person)	have	You (more than one)	have
She, He, or It	has	They	have

Complete each sentence with the correct form of the verb *have*.

1. Rob _____ a garden.

2. I _____ many friends.

3. A flower _____ seeds.

4. The farmer _____ a lot of hay.

5. You _____ a bird feeder.

6. They _____ many books.

7. He _____ some flowers for you.

8. We _____ a lot of plants.

9. Do you _____ a garden?

10. Our neighborhood _____ many stores.

 **Write four sentences with the verb *have*. Share your sentences with a family member.**

Spelling: Long *a* Spelling Patterns

Use with Student Book page 73.

**A. Make a word with a long *a*
spelling pattern.**

1. m _____

2. w _____

3. s _____

4. p _____ d

5. w _____ t

6. _____ t

> ### SPELLING TIP
>
> The letters *ai* and *ay* make the long *a* sound. The letters *eigh* also can make the long *a* sound, as in **neighbor.**

B. Fill in the blanks. Use each word once.

| eight | hay | neigh | neighborhood | trail |

I like to go to the horse farm in my _____ .
I visit the four horses in the field. Then I go into the stable. I pet the four horses inside. There are _____ horses on the farm. The farmer brings _____ to feed the horses. They _____ . Later, I get to ride a horse on the _____ .

 Write about your neighborhood. Use words with *ai*, *ay*, and *eigh*.

_____

_____

 Make a list of six long a words that rhyme. Share your list with a family member.

Name _____ Date _____

Vocabulary

Use with Student Book pages 74–75.

Key Words

- dinner
- well
- roars
- reflection

A. Choose the word that *best* completes each sentence. Write the word.

1. A dog barks, but a lion

_____ .

2. We dug a _____ to find water.

3. When you look in the mirror you see your

_____ .

4. We eat _____ at six o'clock in the evening.

B. Read each clue. Find the key word in the row of letters. Then circle the word.

5. meal in the evening   t w e d i n n e r v t i o n

6. hole with water   p d f l p i t a l w e l l

7. makes a loud noise   p w d w n r o a r s o l p e

8. an image of yourself   d a r e f l e c t i o n h x

C. Answer the questions.

9. What do you like to eat for **dinner**?

_____

10. What **reflection** do you see in the mirror?

_____

11. What do you get from a **well**?

_____

12. Why do you think a lion **roars**?

_____

Academic Words

D. Read each sentence. Write a new sentence using the underlined word.

13. <u>Identify</u> an animal that barks.

_____

14. The trunk and leaves are <u>elements</u> of a tree.

_____

 Write a story using the key words. Share your story with a family member.

Name _____   Date _____

Reader's Companion

Use with Student Book pages 76–79.

The Rabbit and the Lion

Narrator: Rabbit is smart. But one night his foe, Lion, catches him.

Rabbit: Help!

Lion: I have you now, Rabbit! I am going to eat you for dinner!

Rabbit: I am too small. You need a big animal to eat.

Lion: Yes. But you are just the right size for a snack.

Rabbit: Who are you to go around eating rabbits?

Lion: I am king of this forest!

Rabbit: Look at the lion in the well. He says he is king!

Use What You Know

List two things you like to eat for a snack.

1. _____

2. _____

Reading Strategy

What does Rabbit say to try to trick Lion? Underline Rabbit's words.

Comprehension Check

Circle the two words that mean *something to eat.*

39

Use the Strategy

Lion catches Rabbit. What is the first thing Rabbit does? What is the second thing?

_____

_____

_____

Retell It!

Retell this passsage as if you were Rabbit.

_____

_____

_____

_____

Reader's Response

What would you do if Lion caught you?

_____

_____

_____

 **Retell the passage to a family member.**

Name _____ Date _____

Phonics: Long Vowel Pairs (*o, u*)

Use with Student Book page 80.

> The long *o* sound can be spelled *oa* or *oe*.
> The long *u* sound can be spelled *ue* and *ui*.

A. Unscramble the letters to write a word that has a long *o* or long *u* sound. Then circle the letters that spell the long vowel sound.

1. _____   t b a o

2. _____   r i u f t

3. _____   e c u l

4. _____   o t e

B. Use one of the vowel pairs to complete each word in the chart.

Long *o* words	Long *u* words
5. s _____ _____ k	**7.** d _____ _____
6. f _____ _____	**8.** s _____ _____ t

Home-School Connection Add two words to each column in the chart. Share your words with a family member.

41

Comprehension: Events in a Plot

Use with Student Book pages 82–83.

Read the passage. Then underline five important events.

The Lion and the Mouse

Narrator: A lion catches a mouse.

Mouse: Please let me go! Someday I will help you.

Lion: You? What could you do for me?

Narrator: The lion laughed so hard he let the mouse go. The next day, a hunter caught the lion. The hunter tied the lion to a tree.

Lion: ROAR!

Mouse: I will chew through the rope.

Narrator: The mouse chewed through the rope and set the lion free.

Home-School Connection   Write a story. Tell about three events. Tell the events in order. Share your story with a family member.

Name _____ Date _____

Grammar: The Verb *Be*

Use with Student Book page 84.

Subject (one person)	Form of *be*	Subject (more than one person)	Form of *be*
I	am	We	are
You (one person)	are	You (more than one)	are
She, He, or It	is	They	are

Complete each sentence with the correct form of the verb *be*.

1. We _____ happy.

2. A lion _____ a big animal.

3. You _____ very funny.

4. I _____ in school.

5. He _____ on the team.

6. Rabbits _____ fast runners.

7. Turtles _____ very slow.

8. My sister _____ at school.

Home-School Connection Write sentences that describe three members of the family. Use the verb *be*. For example, "I am …," "My mom is…." Share your sentences with a family member.

Spelling: Similar Words

Use with Student Book page 85.

**Read each word and its definition.
Then write the word that *best*
completes each sentence.**

> of – part of something
> off – away from something
> than – used to compare two things
> then – next

1. Hector gets _____ the bus.

2. Josie is taller _____ Eddie.

3. First we cook and _____ we eat.

4. Lion is king _____ the forest.

**Make up a rule to help you remember how to spell two
similar words. Write your rule.**

_____

_____

_____

Name _____ Date _____

Vocabulary

Use with Student Book pages 86–87.

Key Words

clouds

stronger

spiders

webs

brighter

A. Choose the word that *best* completes each sentence. Write the word.

1. The dark _____ moved across the sky.

2. I am _____ than my little brother.

3. Flies were caught in the spider _____.

4. All _____ have eight legs.

5. Sunlight is _____ than moonlight.

B. Unscramble the words.

6. g r e b t h i r _____

7. r i p s d e s _____

8. s l u d o c _____

9. b s e w _____

10. t r g e r s n o _____

45

C. Answer the questions.

11. When are there gray **clouds** in the sky?

_____

12. Why do you think some people do not like **spiders**?

_____

13. Where do you see spider **webs**?

_____

14. How can a person get **stronger**?

_____

15. What shines **brighter** than a flashlight?

_____

Academic Words

D. Read each sentence. Write a new sentence using the underlined word.

16. When you read, look at a new word in <u>context</u>.

_____

17. The <u>final</u> day of the school week is Friday.

_____

 Write another answer for questions 11–15. Share your new answers with a family member.

Name _____ Date _____

Reader's Companion

Use with Student Book pages 88–95.

The Contest

The North Wind took another breath and then she blew very hard. She blew leaves from the trees. She pushed flying birds from the sky. They hid in their nests. The North Wind threw spiders to the ground. She sent their webs flying away.

In the strong wind, it was hard for the woman to stay on her feet. But she never let go of her hat. She held it on her head with both hands.

Use What You Know

List two things you know about the wind.

1. _____

2. _____

Reading Strategy

Underline a sentence that describes how the wind blows.

Comprehension Check

Circle two things the North Wind did when she blew very hard.

47

Use the Strategy

Describe how you picture the North Wind blowing very hard.

_____

_____

_____

Retell It!

Retell this passage as if you were one of the spiders.

_____

_____

_____

_____

Reader's Response

What would you do in such a strong wind?

_____

_____

_____

Retell the passage to a family member.

Name _____   Date _____

Word Analysis: Prefixes and Suffixes

Use with Student Book page 96.

> The prefix *dis* means *not*. The suffix *less* means *without*.

A. Write the word that *best* completes each sentence.

careless   dishonest   dislike   fearless

1. My dad is not afraid of anything. He is _____.

2. It is _____ to tell a lie.

3. The boys are scared of spiders. They _____ them a lot!

4. I did not take care to indent my paragraphs. I was

   _____.

B. Match each word with its definition. Write the letter of the correct answer.

5. _____ disagree   **a.** not trust

6. _____ hopeless   **b.** not obey

7. _____ disobey   **c.** not agree

8. _____ thoughtless   **d.** without hope

9. _____ painless   **e.** without thinking

Home-School Connection Write a sentence using a word with a *dis* prefix. Write a sentence using a word with a *less* suffix. Share your sentences with a family member.

49

Comprehension: Visualize

Use with Student Book pages 98–99.

Read the passage. Then describe pictures you make in your mind.

The Race

Today there is a race in my town. All the children can enter. I want to win the race. I know I am a fast runner. I want to beat Annie. She thinks she is faster than me.

We go to the starting line. The coach says, "Ready, set, go!" I move fast. Soon I am in front of everyone. I can hear someone running close behind me. She catches up, and I see it is Annie.

Annie and I run as fast as we can. We cross the finish line. The coach says, "It is a tie." Annie and I both get medals.

"You are fast," Annie says to me.

"Yes, but you are fast, too," I tell her.

1. What picture do you have of the person telling the story?

_____

_____

2. How do you picture Annie?

_____

_____

 **Ask a family member to tell you a story. Visualize as you listen. Draw a picture of one part of the story.**

Name _____ Date _____

Grammar: Action Verbs
Use with Student Book page 100.

> **Action verbs** show what characters do.

A. Choose the action verb that *best* completes each sentence.

brushes	push	run	sweep	swims

1. The dog _____ in the cold lake.

2. We _____ home after school.

3. I _____ the heavy door open.

4. The boys _____ the floor.

5. Sallie _____ her hair.

B. Read the sentences. Circle the action verbs.

6. My father drives us to the zoo.

7. All the bears jump and roll on the ground.

8. A lion roars at us.

9. The seals splash us.

10. I feed the ducks and pet the goats.

 Write five sentences about a field trip. Use action verbs. Share your sentences with a family member.

51

Spelling: The Long *u* Sound

Use with Student Book page 101.

Read each clue. Write the word that matches the clue. Then circle the letters that spell the long *u* sound.

blue	clue	crew	few	new

1. a group on a space shuttle

_____

2. the color of the sky _____

3. the opposite of *old* _____

4. a hint _____

5. not many _____

✏️ **Write a story using three long *u* words.**

_____

_____

_____

_____

 **Home-School Connection** Make a list of words with the long *u* sound. Share your list with a family member.

Name _____ Date _____

Review

Use with Student Book pages 54–101.

Answer the questions after reading Unit 2. You can go back and reread to help find the answers.

1. In *Birds in the Garden*, what does the family use to make a scarecrow?

   _____

   _____

2. Why does the family make a scarecrow? Circle the letter of the correct answer.

   a. They want to feed the hungry birds.
   b. They hope it will help water the plants.
   c. It will scare the birds out of the garden.
   d. They want to make something for fun.

3. How can birds hurt a garden?

   _____

4. In *The Rabbit and the Lion*, which event happens last? Circle the letter of the correct answer.

   a. Lion says he is king of the forest.
   b. Lion jumps into the well to fight.
   c. Lion roars loudly at his reflection.
   d. Rabbit tells Lion to look in the well.

5. Read these sentences from *The Rabbit and the Lion*.

> **Narrator:** Lion looks into the well. He sees a lion in the water.
> **Rabbit:** Ha! Ha! He thinks his own reflection is another lion!

What is a *reflection*?

_____

_____

6. Describe how you picture the Sun in *The Contest*.

_____

_____

7. Read this sentence from *The Contest*.

> The birds peeked out of their nests.

What does *peeked* mean? Circle the letter of the correct answer.

a. cried   **c.** sang
b. fell   **d.** looked

8. How is the Sun in *The Contest* like Rabbit in *The Rabbit and the Lion*?

_____

_____

 **Tell a family member something new you learned from this unit.**

Name _____   Date _____

Vocabulary
Use with Student Book pages 112–113.

A. **Choose the word that *best* completes each sentence. Write the word.**

1. The _____ flies from flower to flower.

2. A _____ builds

   a _____ around itself.

3. When a _____ grows up, it is a frog.

4. In autumn, the _____ will turn red.

5. The baby birds _____ out of their shells.

B. **Read each clue. Find the key word in the row of letters. Then circle the word.**

6. part of a plant   t w s d f n t e l e a f m n

7. insect with a long body
   and large wings   p e b u t t e r f l y p e

8. insect with a round body
   and many legs   c a c a t e r p i l l a r e g

9. baby frog   s e r f u t e t a d p o l e

10. come out of an egg   d h a t c h j r t i o n h x

55

C. Answer the following questions.

11. What does a **butterfly** look like?

_____

12. Why does a **caterpillar** build a **chrysalis**?

_____

13. How does a **tadpole** become a frog?

_____

14. When is a **leaf** green?

_____

15. What animals **hatch** from eggs?

_____

Academic Words

D. Read each sentence. Write a new sentence using the underlined word.

16. The butterfly goes through a <u>process</u> as it grows.

_____

17. In the <u>initial</u> step, the butterfly is an egg.

_____

 **Home-School Connection** Draw the life cycle of a butterfly. Write labels and captions. Share your picture with a family member.

Name _____ Date _____

Reader's Companion

Use with Student Book pages 114–117.

How Do They Grow?

A butterfly must find a place to lay eggs. A leaf is a good place.

Soon an egg will hatch. A tiny caterpillar crawls out. The caterpillar starts to eat right away. It munches on plants.

Next, the caterpillar builds a chrysalis around itself. The chrysalis sticks to a tree branch. It hangs there and does not move. But changes happen inside.

Then the butterfly breaks out of the chrysalis. It spreads its wings. It is ready to fly.

Use What You Know

List two insects you see outside.

1. _____

2. _____

Reading Strategy

Find four steps in a butterfly's life. Write the numbers 1, 2, 3, and 4 next to each step.

Comprehension Check

Where does the butterfly lay eggs? Circle the answer.

Use the Strategy

What does the caterpillar do?

_____

_____

_____

Retell It!

Tell how the butterfly grows and changes. Explain the steps as if you are the teacher in a science class.

_____

_____

_____

_____

Reader's Response

Think of different butterflies that you have seen. What did they look like?

_____

_____

_____

 **Retell the passage to a family member.**

Name _____   Date _____

Phonics: Digraphs *ch, sh, th*

Use with Student Book page 118.

> The letters *ch*, *sh*, and *th* are **digraphs**.
> Each digraph stands for one sound.

A. Circle the digraph in each word.

1. chick

2. ship

3. gather

4. munch

5. things

B. Add *ch*, *sh*, or *th* to make a word.

6. _____ _____ o e

7. a n o _____ _____ e r

8. _____ _____ a n k s

9. t o u _____ _____

10. r u _____ _____

Think of two more words each with *ch*, *sh*, and *th*.
Read your words to a family member.

59

Comprehension: Steps in a Process

Use with Student Book pages 120–121.

Read each passage. Then number the steps in the correct order.

Life Cycle of a Robin

First, the mother robin lays eggs in a nest. Next, the eggs hatch. The babies have no feathers. They stay in the nest. The mother brings them food. Then the young robins grow feathers and learn to fly. They leave the nest and fly away.

_____ The eggs hatch.

_____ The mother robin lays eggs.

_____ The young robins grow feathers and learn to fly.

_____ The babies have no feathers. They stay in the nest.

Life Cycle of a Frog

First, a frog lays eggs in water. Soon, the eggs hatch. Tiny tadpoles come out of the eggs. These tadpoles live in water and have no legs. One day, they start growing legs. After ten weeks, the legs are big. The tadpole can go onto land. The tadpole has become a frog.

_____ Tadpoles start growing legs.

_____ A frog lays eggs in water.

_____ The tadpole has become a frog.

_____ Tadpoles come out of the eggs.

 **Home-School Connection** Tell a family member what you did after school today. Tell the steps in order.

Name _____ Date _____

Grammar: Subject-Verb Agreement

Use with Student Book page 122.

> In a sentence, the verbs must agree with the subject.
> **Agreement** means that they go together.

Read each sentence. Circle the correct form of the verb.

1. Frogs (hop / hops).

2. I (swim / swims) very well.

3. He (like / likes) to walk in the park.

4. The flowers (grow / grows) quickly.

5. A chrysalis (hang / hangs) from a branch.

6. Caterpillars (munch / munches) on leaves.

7. She (play / plays) with frogs a lot!

8. The insect (lay / lays) its eggs in water.

9. We (hike / hikes) in the summer.

10. One bear (eat / eats) fish from our pond.

 Write three sentences about an animal. Use the correct form of the verb. Share your sentences with a family member.

Spelling: Spelling with *tch*

Use with Student Book page 123.

Add *tch* to make each word.

SPELLING TIP

The *ch* sound may be spelled *tch* when it is in a one-syllable word with a short vowel.

1. A hu_____ is a home for rabbits.

2. My dad will make a ba_____ of cookies.

3. Pi_____ the ball to the batter.

4. Can you ma_____ the words and pictures?

5. I will look at my wa_____ to see what time it is.

6. It rained hard. The di_____ is full of water.

7. Let's wa_____ the soccer game.

8. Can you draw or ske_____ the butterfly?

Write a story about a child who catches a big fish. Use words with *tch* in your story.

_____

_____

_____

 **Read the sentences to a family member. Talk about what each word means.**

Name _____ Date _____

Vocabulary

Use with Student Book pages 124–125.

Key Words

camels

amazing

habits

caves

plains

A. **Choose the word that *best* completes each sentence. Write the word.**

1. A giraffe is an _____ animal.

2. Most _____ live in the desert.

3. The dog's _____ are barking and chasing its tail.

4. Zebras in Africa live on the _____.

5. Bears live in dark _____.

B. **Unscramble the words.**

6. v s e a c _____

7. z a i m n g a _____

8. s p i a n l _____

9. m e l s c a _____

10. b i h a s t _____

C. Answer the questions.

11. What animals live on the **plains**?

_____

12. What **habits** do you have?

_____

13. What animals live in **caves**?

_____

14. What is the most **amazing** animal you have ever seen?

_____

15. How many humps do **camels** have on their backs?

_____

Academic Words

D. Read each sentence. Write a new sentence using the underlined word.

16. One <u>method</u> for studying is to do the hard parts first.

_____

17. A beak is a <u>feature</u> of a bird.

_____

 **Tell a family member about your favorite animals. Use the key words.**

Name _____ Date _____

Reader's Companion

Use with Student Book pages 126–129.

Animals at Home

Animals live all over the world
in many kinds of homes.
Bats live in caves, monkeys in trees,
and camels in desert zones.

Hippos live their lives in mud
and polar bears in snow.
Zebras live out on the plains
where lions come and go.

Use What You Know

List three animals you know.

1. _____

2. _____

3. _____

Reading Strategy

List two things you think monkeys do in trees.

1. _____

2. _____

Comprehension Check

Where do hippos live? Circle the answer in the poem.

MARK the TEXT

Use the Strategy

Why do you think different animals live in different kinds of homes?

_____

_____

_____

Retell It!

Retell the first four lines of the passage as an interview. Your interview should include questions and answers.

_____

_____

_____

_____

Reader's Response

Choose one of the habitats from the passage. Think of two other animals that live in this habitat.

_____

_____

_____

Retell the passage to a family member.

Name _____ Date _____

Phonics: Consonant Clusters
Use with Student Book page 130.

> In **consonant clusters,** the sounds of both
> letters blend together.

r-blends	*l*-blends	*s*-blends
br, cr, dr, fr, gr, pr, tr	bl, cl, fl, gl, pl, sl	sc, sk, sm, sn, sp, st, sw

Add an *r*-blend, *s*-blend, or an *l*-blend to make a word.

1. _____ oom

2. _____ ile

3. _____ ee

4. _____ ape

5. _____ ay

6. _____ ess

7. _____ eep

8. _____ ip

9. _____ ue

10. _____ im

Write three sentences using some of the words you made.
Share your sentences with a family member.

Comprehension: Inferences

Use with Student Book pages 132–133.

Read the passage. Put a check by the sentence that *best* tells what you can figure out by reading.

Parents

Mother and father birds have a lot to do. First they have to build the nest. Then they have to sit on the eggs until they hatch. But their work is not done. Baby birds need to be fed. The parents bring the babies food to eat. Sometimes people or animals get too close to the nest. The parent birds will squawk to keep them away.

_____ Lots of animals like to eat birds.

_____ Birds do a good job of caring for their young.

_____ Birds do not care much for their young.

_____ Birds teach their babies how to fly.

 With a family member, make a list of birds and other animals you have seen.

68

Name _____ Date _____

Grammar: Types of Sentences

Use with Student Book page 134.

> A **declarative sentence** tells something.
> An **interrogative sentence** asks a question.
> An **imperative sentence** tells someone to do something.
> An **exclamatory sentence** expresses strong feeling.

A. Read each sentence. Then write the type of sentence.

1. _____ Bears sleep all winter.

2. _____ You are so funny!

3. _____ Do camels live in deserts?

4. _____ Look at that amazing animal.

B. Write a sentence using each group of words.

5. interrogative sentence: live / city / you / a / do / in

_____

6. imperative sentence: me / about / book / give / animals / the

_____

7. declarative sentence: faster / turtles / rabbits / than / are

_____

 Write an exclamatory sentence. Read your sentence to a family member.

69

Spelling: Adding *-ing*

Use with Student Book page 135.

**Change the underlined word to
the *-ing* form. Rewrite each sentence.**

1. I am <u>make</u> a poster about animals.

_____

2. Are you <u>share</u> your toys?

_____

3. The bears are <u>live</u> in caves.

_____

4. We are <u>hike</u> in the hills.

_____

5. She is <u>write</u> a letter to her grandmother.

_____

**Write two sentences about what animals do.
Use words that drop a silent *e* to add *-ing*.**

_____

_____

Share your sentences with a family member. Explain the rule.

70

Name _____ Date _____

Vocabulary

Use with Student Book pages 136–137.

Key Words

insect

habitats

camouflage

prey

patterns

moth

A. Choose the word that *best* completes each sentence. Write the word.

1. Some butterflies have colorful

   _____ on their wings.

2. Rivers and lakes are

   _____ for fish.

3. A bird is a cat's _____ .

4. A _____ looks a lot like a butterfly.

5. That _____ looks like a stick!

6. Rabbits use _____ to stay safe.

B. Match each word with its definition. Write the letter of the correct answer.

7. _____ habitats   **a.** what animals use to hide

8. _____ moth   **b.** animals' homes

9. _____ camouflage   **c.** animal that other animals eat

10. _____ prey   **d.** small flying insect

71

C. Answer the questions.

11. What are **habitats**?

_____

12. What do animals use **camouflage** for?

_____

13. How many legs does an **insect** have?

_____

14. How do **patterns** help the pepper **moth**?

_____

15. How can animals that are **prey** stay safe?

_____

Academic Words

D. Read each sentence. Write a new sentence using the underlined word.

16. The <u>function</u> of a camera is to take pictures.

_____

17. The bird's <u>reaction</u> to a noise is to fly away.

_____

Explain to a family member how animals use camouflage to stay safe.

Name _____ Date _____

Reader's Companion

Use with Student Book pages 138–141.

Can You See Them?

Arctic foxes live where the weather is very cold. They can change color. In summer, the foxes are brown. In winter, they are white.

A tawny frogmouth is a bird. It sits very still in a tree. It waits for prey to come near. Then it pounces!

Patterns help this moth stay safe. Look at the big spots on the moth's wings. They look like a large animal's eyes. Predators stay away from this insect.

A Bengal tiger is a very large cat. It's hard for a big animal to hide. But the tiger has stripes. When it rests in the forest, its stripes blend in with the plants.

Use What You Know

List two things you know about animals.

1. _____

2. _____

Reading Strategy

MARK the TEXT

Find three causes and effects in the passage. Write C over the cause. Write E over the effect.

Comprehension Check

What is a tawny frogmouth?

_____

_____

_____

73

Use the Strategy

Why do you think Arctic foxes are a different color in summer than in winter?

_____

_____

_____

Retell It!

Retell one part of this passage as if you were a park ranger telling about an animal in your park.

_____

_____

_____

_____

Reader's Response

Which of the animals in this passage would you like to learn more about? Why?

_____

_____

_____

Retell the passage to a family member.

Name _____ Date _____

Word Analysis: Compounds Words

Use with Student Book page 142.

Compound words are made up of two smaller words.

something	classroom	birthday
some / thing	class / room	birth / day

Read each clue. Then use the words to write the compound word.

back	boat	bow	brush	earth	grass
hopper	house	lawn	mower	rain	set
sun	tooth	worm	yard		

1. you use it to brush your teeth _____

2. an insect that can jump very high _____

3. it cuts grass _____

4. a home that is on the water _____

5. you might see this after it rains _____

6. this lives underground _____

7. this is behind a house _____

8. this happens at the end of a day _____

 **Think of five compound words. Use each one in a sentence. Share your sentences with a family member.**

75

Comprehension: Cause and Effect

Use with Student Book pages 144–145.

Read each passage. Write the cause and effect.

Jarrett Goes to School

It was a nice day. Jarrett decided to ride his bike to school. On the way to school, he rode over a nail. One of his tires went flat. Jarrett couldn't ride the bike with a flat tire. He had to walk the rest of the way to school. He got there ten minutes late.

Cause _____

Effect _____

Allison and Rusty

Allison has a pet puppy, Rusty. Rusty can run very fast. Allison taught Rusty to come when she called his name. One day Rusty ran away. Allison could not find him. Then she called his name. Rusty came back.

Cause _____

Effect _____

 **Explain cause and effect to a family member. Give an example from the selection.**

Name _____   Date _____

Grammar: Complete Sentences
Use with Student Book page 146.

> **Complete sentences** begin with a capital letter and end with a period (.), a question mark (?), or an exclamation point (!).

Read each group of words. Rewrite to make each one a complete sentence.

1. farmers put scarecrows in fields

_____

2. do insects have six legs or eight legs

_____

3. that was an amazing movie

_____

4. i have a birdhouse in my garden

_____

5. when is your birthday

_____

Write five more sentences. Start each sentence with a capital letter. Use the correct punctuation mark at the end. Read your sentences to a family member.

Spelling: Compound Words

Use with Student Book page 147.

Unscramble the smaller words.
Write the compound word.

1. n w e s   p p r a e   _____

2. s s r o c   k l w a   _____

3. m e s o   g h n i t   _____

4. c r e a s   w r o c   _____

5. r i a   n l e p a   _____

6. n s u   s e r i   _____

7. g r e n f i   l n i a   _____

8. y d a   r e m a d   _____

Write a story. Use three of the compound words.

_____

_____

_____

_____

Share your story with a family member. Point out the compound words.

Name _____ Date _____

Review

Use with Student Book pages 106–147.

Answer the questions after reading Unit 3. You can go back and reread to help find the answers.

1. In *How Do They Grow?*, what steps does a frog go through as it grows? Circle the letter of the correct answer.

   a. tadpole, egg, frog
   b. egg, caterpillar, frog
   c. egg, tadpole, frog
   d. egg, chrysalis, tadpole

2. Where does a tadpole live?

   _____

   _____

3. Read these sentences from the selection.

   > Soon an egg will hatch. A tiny caterpillar crawls out.

   What does *hatch* mean? Circle the letter of the correct answer.

   a. close up   c. crawl out
   b. break open   d. fly away

4. What step is the same for both frogs and butterflies?

   _____

   _____

79

5. In *Animals at Home,* what animals live in the ocean? Circle the letter of the correct answer.

    a. bats, monkeys, and camels
    b. crocodiles, fish, and snakes
    c. cats, dogs, and rabbits
    d. whales, sharks, and jellyfish

6. Read this sentence from the poem.

> Zebras live out on the plains where lions come and go.

    Zebra are lion's prey. What do you think happens when zebras and lions are together on the plains?

_____

_____

7. Read these sentences from *Can You See Them?* Then write the cause and the effect.

> The cottontail rabbit hides in some leaves on the ground in the forest. It must hide from predators.

    Cause _____

    Effect _____

8. What is a *habitat?* Circle the letter of the correct answer.

    a. an animal's home   **c.** a camouflage
    b. an animal's habit   **d.** a predator

 Home-School Connection Tell a family member something new you learned from this unit.

Name _____ Date _____

Vocabulary

Use with Student Book pages 158–159.

A. Choose the word that *best* completes each sentence. Write the word.

1. The _____ made cookies to sell at the fair.

2. Many children will _____ old toys to sell.

3. Jess and Kim rode their _____ to the fair.

4. They wore _____ to be safe.

B. Unscramble the words. Then write a definition for each word.

5. n d a o e t _____

_____

6. i c l b e s c y _____

_____

7. e m s l h e t _____

_____

8. t e n o e u r l v s _____

_____

C. Answer the questions.

9. Why do people **donate** old clothes and toys?

_____

10. Why should people wear **helmets** when they ride bikes?

_____

11. How do the school **volunteers** help children?

_____

12. Where can people ride **bicycles**?

_____

Academic Words

D. Read each sentence. Write a new sentence using the underlined word.

13. Bikes for the World can <u>benefit</u> people who do not have bicycles.

_____

14. Bikes for the World does <u>significant</u> work.

_____

Make up your own questions using the key words. Ask a family member to answer your questions.

Name _____ Date _____

Reader's Companion

Use with Student Book pages 160–167.

On Your Bike, Get Set, Donate!

Young people can help, too. Joshua started fixing bikes when he was twelve years old. He gave them to children who did not have bicycles.

Joshua got started when his own bike broke. He had an idea. He would learn how to fix it himself. Soon, neighbors were bringing old bikes to Joshua's house. He repaired them. Now other children have new bikes.

Use What You Know

List two places where you can ride bicycles.

1. _____

2. _____

Reading Strategy

MARK the TEXT

Read the passage. In the second paragraph, circle Joshua's problem. Underline the sentence that shows how he solved the problem.

Comprehension Check

MARK the TEXT

Who did Joshua give bikes to? Draw a box around the answer.

Use the Strategy

What problem did Joshua solve when he fixed his neighbors' old bikes?

_____

_____

_____

Retell It!

Retell the passage as if you are Joshua.

_____

_____

_____

_____

Reader's Response

What would you like to do to help people?

_____

_____

_____

 Summarize the passage for a family member.

Name _____ Date _____

Word Analysis: Ending -ed

Use with Student Book page 168.

> Add **-ed** to a word to show something happened in the past.

A. Write the past tense of each verb by adding the -ed ending.

1. load   _____

2. fix   _____

3. repair   _____

4. hunt   _____

5. learn   _____

B. Read each sentence. Underline the words with **-ed** where the ending added a syllable. Circle the words with **-ed** where the ending did not add a syllable.

6. The spaceship landed on the moon.

7. I stacked the cups on the shelf.

8. Did you like how the movie ended?

9. We painted pictures in art class.

10. Jenna looked out the window.

Home-School Connection   **Write five sentences using words ending in -ed.**

85

Comprehension: Problems and Solutions

Use with Student Book pages 170–171.

Read the passage. Complete the Problem and Solution Chart.

Jamie's New Bike

Jamie's neighbor, Kara, got a bicycle. Jamie watched Kara ride it around the block.

"I wish I had a bicycle," said Jamie.

"You can have my old bike," said Jamie's big sister, Lauren. "But the front tire is flat."

Jamie had an idea. He went to Kara's house. He asked her, "Do you have a tire pump?"

"Yes," said Kara. "It is in the garage."

The two friends found the tire pump. They pumped up the front tire until it was full. Now Jamie has a new bike, too. Jamie and Kara can ride their bikes together.

Problem	Solution

 With a family member, write about a problem you had. Tell how you solved it.

Name _____ Date _____

Grammar: Pronouns

Use with Student Book page 172.

> **Pronouns** take the place of nouns.
>
> The pronouns *I, you, he, she, it, we,* and *they* are subject pronouns. They tell who or what does the action.
>
> The pronouns *me, you, him, her, it, us,* and *them* are object pronouns. They tell who or what receives the action.

A. Circle the correct pronoun in each sentence.

1. Will you teach [I, me] how to ride?

2. [Us, We] donated a cake for the bake sale.

3. I brought [she, her] to the race.

4. [He, Him] and I are best friends!

B. Write pronouns to take the place of the underlined words.

5. <u>Mrs. Walton</u> takes care of <u>the girl</u>. _____ _____

6. Will <u>the man</u> help <u>those children</u>? _____ _____

7. <u>Susie and I</u> have a gift for <u>Joey</u>. _____ _____

Circle different pronouns in a newspaper article. Share your work with a family member.

Spelling: Adding *-es* to Verbs

Use with Student Book page 173.

Read each sentence. Circle the correct spelling of the verb.

> **SPELLING TIP**
>
> To make verbs agree with a singular subject, add *-s*. For verbs that end in *x, s, ch, sh*, and *z*, add *-es*.

1. The boy (mix / mixes) water and sand.

2. The girl (wish / wishes) she had a horse.

3. She (reach / reaches) for her hat.

4. The bee (buzz / buzzes) by the flower.

5. Sari (touch / touches) the door.

6. The woman (push / pushes) the door open.

7. The man (guess / guesses) the answer.

8. Jill (relax / relaxes) after her race.

 Write three sentences using verbs with *-es* added.

_____

_____

_____

_____

 **With a family member, think of one more verb for each ending, *x, s, ch, sh*, and *z*.**

88

Name _____ Date _____

Vocabulary
Use with Student Book pages 174–175.

A. **Choose the word that *best* completes each sentence. Write the word.**

1. Some _____ study animals in their habitats.

2. A bird breaks out of its egg

   by _____.

3. A hammer is a _____ used to build something.

4. A scientist's laboratory may be called a _____.

5. The photograph is _____ that the cat climbed a tree.

B. **Match each word with its definition. Write the letter of the correct answer.**

6. _____ instinct

7. _____ tool

8. _____ lab

9. _____ scientists

10. _____ proof

a. facts that show something is true

b. place where experiments are done

c. ability you are born with

d. object or machine people use to do work

e. people who study the natural world

C. Answer the questions.

11. What does **instinct** help animals to do?

_____

12. Where can **scientists** do their work?

_____

13. What might you find in a **lab**?

_____

14. What **tool** can you use to cut paper?

_____

15. What gives **proof** that you are alive?

_____

Academic Words

D. Read each sentence. Write a new sentence using the underlined word.

16. Some scientists have a <u>theory</u> that crows can make tools.

_____

17. The scientists <u>conclude</u> that some crows can make tools.

_____

 Use the key words to write a paragraph about what scientists do. Share your paragraph with a family member.

Name _____ Date _____

Reader's Companion

Use with Student Book pages 176–181.

Scientists and Crows

Do you ever watch crows? You may see crows fly over trees. You may see a crow sit on a power line. Maybe you hear crows call, "Caw! Caw! Caw!"

Scientists watch crows, too. They watch what crows do in their habitat. They also study crows in labs. Scientists study crows to learn more about them.

Use the Strategy

Why do scientists study crows?

_____

_____

How do scientists study crows?

_____

_____

_____

Retell It!

Summarize the passage as if you are a scientist.

_____

_____

_____

_____

_____

Reader's Response

What animals do you like to watch? Why?

_____

_____

_____

 **Home-School Connection** Summarize the passage for a family member.

92

Name _____ Date _____

Phonics: *r*-Controlled Vowels *ir, er, ur*
Use with Student Book page 182.

> The letter *r* after a vowel gives the vowel a new sound. The letters *ir, er*, and *ur* usually have the same vowel sound.

Read each clue. Write the word that matches the clue. Then circle the letters that make the *r*-controlled vowel sound.

burn	curved	first	girl
herd	shirt	turn	verb

1. not straight   _____

2. my little sister   _____

3. an action word   _____

4. a piece of clothing   _____

5. number one   _____

6. group of deer   _____

7. what fires do   _____

8. go in a circle   _____

 **With a family member, list two more words for each *r*-controlled sound.**

93

Comprehension: Main Idea and Details

Use with Student Book pages 184–185.

Read the passage. Then fill in the Main Idea and Details Chart.

Crows Work Together

I think crows are birds that work together. I watched two crows build a nest. They each gathered sticks and grass to build it. Then the mother sat on the eggs. The father crow brought her food. Later, three baby crows hatched. When the mother went to get food, the father sat near the nest to guard the babies.

Hawks may eat baby crows. If a hawk comes near, the adult crows team up and chase him away. I think it's really neat how the crows work together.

Main Idea

Supporting Details

Watch some birds with a family member. List details that you see.
Write a paragraph about the birds.

Name _____ Date _____

Grammar: Possessives

Use with Student Book page 186.

> **Possessives** show what someone or something has.
> They can be nouns or pronouns.

A. Read each sentence. Circle the possessive nouns.

1. We gave away all of the cat's kittens.

2. The first singer's song was beautiful.

3. The tree's fruit fell on the ground.

4. The artists' paintings were on the wall.

B. Read each sentence. Choose the correct possessive pronoun. Write the word.

her	his	its	my	your

5. Please give me _____ ball back.

6. The girl sang, and _____ song was beautiful.

7. Where did you put _____ backpack?

8. The tiger hunts for _____ food.

9. My brother can fix _____ own bike.

 **Read a story aloud to a family member. Together, listen to hear possessive nouns or pronouns.**

Spelling: Personal Word List

Use with Student Book page 187.

Read each word. Write its definition using a dictionary.

SPELLING TIP

Keep a personal word list. Write words that are hard for you to spell.

1. experiment

_____

_____

2. observe

_____

_____

3. behavior

_____

_____

✎ **Use the words. Write a story about a scientist who studies an animal.**

_____

_____

_____

List ten words for your personal word list. They should be words you want to remember how to spell. Read the list to a family member.

Name _____ Date _____

Vocabulary
Use with Student Book pages 188–189.

A. Choose the word that *best* completes each sentence. Write the word.

Key Words

- costume
- robe
- painting
- teepee
- mask
- quilt

1. The grandmother made a

_____ to cover the bed.

2. The actor wore a _____
to hide his face.

3. A _____ is a kind of tent.

4. In art class, Jess made a _____ using
watercolors.

5. The queen wore a _____ around her
shoulders.

6. The actor wore a _____ to look like a king.

B. Read each clue. Write the word that matches the clue.

7. blanket made from pieces of cloth _____

8. clothes that make you look like someone else

_____

9. something that covers your face _____

10. painted picture _____

97

C. Answer the following questions.

11. Where might you find a **teepee**?

_____

12. When does someone wear a **costume**?

_____

13. Why might someone wear a **mask**?

_____

14. Who wears a **robe**?

_____

15. What would you like to make a **painting** of?

_____

Academic Words

D. Read each sentence. Write a new sentence using the underlined word.

16. Please <u>respond</u> to the question.

_____

17. It is a <u>tradition</u> to make Mother's Day cards.

_____

 Draw a picture that shows or describes each key word. Ask a family member to help you label your drawings.

Name _____ Date _____

Reader's Companion
Use with Student Book pages 190–193.

A Story to Tell

Lakota people made this dream catcher using string, beads, and feathers. Lakota legends say that Spider Woman made the first dream catcher. She told them that the web would catch bad dreams and keep them away. Good dreams could come in through the hole in the center.

Use What You Know

Name one thing you can make with beads and string.

_____

_____

Reading Strategy MARK the TEXT

Circle the sentence that tells what the dream catcher does with bad dreams.

Comprehension Check MARK the TEXT

Underline the sentence that explains what happens to the good dreams.

Use the Strategy

Write a question you can ask to better understand the passage.
Then answer your question.

_____

_____

_____

_____

Retell It!

Retell the passage as if you are Spider Woman.

_____

_____

_____

_____

Reader's Response

Tell about a good dream you had.

_____

_____

_____

Summarize the passage for a family member.

Name _____ Date _____

Phonics: Hard and Soft c

Use with Student Book page 194.

> A **hard c** has a *k* sound.
>
> A **soft c** has an *s* sound.

because	celebrate	center	circle
come	cow	cut	fancy

A. Choose a word with a hard *c* to complete each sentence. Write the word.

1. The _____ eats grass in a field.

2. Please _____ to the park with me.

3. I clean my room _____ I like to be neat.

4. My dad _____ my hair.

B. Choose a word with a soft *c* to complete each sentence. Write the word.

5. My family likes to _____ special days.

6. Draw a _____ around the right answer.

7. That is a _____ costume!

8. There is a hole in the _____ of the web.

 **Home-School Connection** With a family member, list three more words with a hard *c*, and three more words with a soft *c*.

Comprehension: Ask Questions

Use with Student Book pages 196–197.

Read the passage. Then answer the questions below.

The Maya

The Maya live in Mexico and Central America. They have lived there for many years. Over 1,000 years ago, the Maya built cities in the rain forest. The cities are now ruins. Ruins are parts of buildings that have fallen down.

An old Mayan city could be very big. There were many large buildings. The Mayan people carved pictures on the walls of their buildings. Also, there was a court where people played a ball game. Today, Mayan people still play this ball game.

1. When did the Maya build cities in the rain forest?

_____

2. What has happened to the cities?

_____

_____

3. What things were in a Mayan city?

_____

_____

 **Share the questions with a family member. Tell why asking these questions helps you understand the passage.**

Name _____ Date _____

Grammar: Adjectives and Articles

Use with Student Book page 198.

> **Adjectives** describe or tell more about
> a noun. The words *the, a,* and *an* are
> articles. **Articles** point out nouns.

**Read each sentence. Underline each adjective.
Circle each article.**

1. The city was built on a rocky cliff.

2. My best friend wore an orange cap and a shiny raincoat.

3. We followed a long, narrow path into the woods.

4. Did grandmother use an old loom to weave the colorful rug?

5. A buffalo is a strong and powerful animal.

6. The painting had white daisies and red roses.

7. They slept in a teepee during warm weather.

8. She wore a scary mask in the play.

9. Pearl carved an animal shape into the brown rock.

10. Does your dog have a loud bark?

 **Write five sentences. Each sentence should have at least one adjective and one article.**

103

Spelling: The Letter *q*

Use with Student Book page 199.

Read each clue. Write the word that matches the clue.

quack	quarter	quiet
square	squeak	squeeze

1. to hold something tightly _____

2. sound a duck makes _____

3. shape with four sides _____

4. not loud _____

5. twenty-five cents _____

6. sound a mouse makes _____

Write a story about a queen who makes a quilt. See how many words with *qu* you can put in the story.

_____

_____

_____

_____

With a family member, read the dictionary meanings for *squid*, *liquid*, and *sequoia*.

Name _____ Date _____

Review

Use with Student Book pages 152–199.

Answer the questions after reading Unit 4. You can go back and reread to help find the answers.

1. Name two countries in Africa that groups donate bikes to in *On Your Bike, Get Set, Donate!* Circle the letter of the correct answer.

   a. Togo and Kenya
   b. Ghana and Nigeria
   c. Kenya and Nigeria
   d. Togo and Ghana

2. People throw away their old bikes. What is a solution to this problem?

   _____

   _____

3. Why does Bicycle Exchange teach bicycle safety to children?

   _____

   _____

4. In *Scientists* and *Crows*, you learn that crows in Japan crack walnuts. List one way that the crows crack the walnuts.

   _____

   _____

5. Read these sentences from *Scientists and Crows*.

> Scientists know that birds do many things by instinct.
> For example, they learn to fly by instinct.

What does *instinct* mean? Circle the letter of the correct answer.

a. something you are born knowing how to do
b. something your parents teach you how to do
c. something you learn by solving a problem
d. something only crows know how to do

6. In *A Story to Tell*, how does Mateo make a rug?

_____

_____

_____

7. Native Americans in California made a basket that shows a rattlesnake trying to catch a toad. Why do you think the basket shows these two animals? Circle the letter of the correct answer.

a. The people made the basket to hold toads.
b. The people often saw the rattlesnake and toad.
c. The people made the basket to hold rattlesnakes.
d. The people had never seen a snake or a toad.

 Tell a family member something new you learned in this unit.

Name _____ Date _____

Vocabulary

Use with Student Book pages 210–211.

Key Words

sphere

craters

billions

planets

rotates

continents

A. Choose the word that *best* completes each sentence. Write the word.

1. Earth _____ on its axis.

2. Earth has the shape of a

   _____ .

3. Earth and Mars are _____ in our solar system.

4. Africa is one of Earth's _____ .

5. There are _____ of stars in the sky.

6. There are many _____ , or large holes, on the moon.

B. Unscramble the words.

7. t r a s t o e   _____

8. n n n t t o c i e s   _____

9. r e h e p s   _____

10. s t e l n a p   _____

107

C. Answer the questions.

11. Why does a globe have the shape of a **sphere**?

_____

12. Where could you find **billions** of drops of water?

_____

13. How many **planets** are in the solar system?

_____

14. Where could you see **craters**?

_____

15. What happens when Earth **rotates** around its axis?

_____

Academic Words

D. Read each sentence. Write a new sentence using the underlined word.

16. The <u>label</u> identifies Earth in the solar system.

_____

17. The <u>location</u> of Earth is third planet from the sun.

_____

 Use each key word in a sentence. Share your sentences with a family member.

Name _____ Date _____

Reader's Companion

Use with Student Book pages 212–217.

Earth and Beyond

What is the sun?

The sun is a star. Earth and the other planets orbit the sun.

Why does the sun look so big and bright?

It looks big and bright because it is closer than any other star. The sun is so bright that we can't see other stars during the day.

The sun is always glowing. So why is the sky dark at night?

Earth rotates every 24 hours. When our side of Earth faces the sun, we have day. When our side faces away from the sun, we have night.

Why is the sun so important?

The sun warms and lights Earth.

Can people visit the sun?

No! The sun is too hot.

Use What You Know

List three things that you can see in space.

1. _____

2. _____

3. _____

Reading Strategy

MARK the TEXT

When is it day on Earth? When is it night? Review the text. Underline the answers.

Comprehension Check

MARK the TEXT

Why can't people visit the sun? Circle the answer.

Use the Strategy

Why does the sun look so big and bright?

_____

_____

_____

Retell It!

Pretend you are a teacher on a space shuttle flight. You are teaching a science lesson from space! Summarize the passage.

_____

_____

_____

_____

_____

Reader's Response

Where would you like to go in space if you were an astronaut? Why?

_____

_____

_____

Home-School Connection   **Summarize the passage for a family member.**

Name _____ Date _____

Word Analysis: Synonyms and Antonyms

Use with Student Book page 218.

> **Synonyms** are words that have the same or similar meanings.
> **Antonyms** are words that have opposite meanings.

A. Match each word with its synonym. Write the letter of the correct answer.

1. _____ begin   **a.** stone

2. _____ final   **b.** start

3. _____ great   **c.** important

4. _____ benefit   **d.** last

5. _____ rock   **e.** help

B. Write the antonym for each word.

| awake | fast | heavy | old | short |

6. new   _____

7. tall   _____

8. slow   _____

9. asleep   _____

10. light   _____

 **With a family member, think of a synonym and an antonym for** *happy, little,* **and** *pretty.*

Comprehension: Review

Use with Student Book pages 220–221.

Read the passage. Then review the passage. Answer the questions.

Shining Stars

Look at the sky at night. The tiny lights are stars. Each star is many times bigger than Earth. Stars look small because they are far away.

Stars begin as clouds of gas and dust. Over time, these clouds get hotter and hotter. The gases begin to burn. As the young star heats up, it starts to shine.

1. How big are stars?

_____

2. Why do stars look so tiny?

_____

3. What are stars made of?

_____

 Tell a family member one more thing you learned about the sun and stars.

Name _____   Date _____

Grammar: Present Tense Verbs

Use with Student Book page 222.

> **Present tense verbs** name actions that happen now.

Complete each sentence. Use the present tense form of each verb.

give	live	look	orbit
rotate	see	shine	travel

1. The sun _____ .

2. No one _____ on the moon.

3. Astronauts _____ into space.

4. Astronauts _____ at Earth from space.

5. The sun _____ us light.

6. All the planets _____ the sun.

7. Earth _____ on its axis.

8. We _____ stars in the night sky.

 **Write three sentences telling what people in your family like to eat. Use present tense verbs.**

113

Spelling: Words with *ph*

Use with Student Book page 223.

SPELLING TIP

In some words, the /f/ sound is spelled *ph*.

| alphabet | elephant | phone |
| photographer | sphere | |

Read each clue. Write the word that matches the clue.

1. someone who takes a picture _____

2. big animal with a trunk _____

3. equipment you use for talking _____

4. letters that make up words _____

5. round like a ball _____

Write three sentences. Use words with *ph*.

_____

_____

_____

Home-School Connection Share your sentences with a family member.

Name _____ Date _____

Vocabulary
Use with Student Book pages 224–225.

Key Words

space shuttle

flight

satellite

observe

spacewalks

A. **Choose the word that *best* completes each sentence. Write the word.**

1. Astronauts wear spacesuits when they take

   _____ .

2. A space shuttle blasts off to begin its

   _____ .

3. A robot helps scientists _____ the surface of Mars.

4. Astronauts ride the _____ to get to the space station.

5. A _____ helps televisions work.

B. **Match each word with its definition. Write the letter of the correct answer.**

6. _____ space shuttle   **a.** to look closely at

7. _____ flight   **b.** a trip in a space vehicle

8. _____ satellite   **c.** human-made object that orbits Earth

9. _____ spacewalks   **d.** spacecraft that can travel into space and back to Earth

10. _____ observe   **e.** trips made by an astronaut outside a spacecraft

C. Answer the questions.

11. Where does the **space shuttle** travel?

_____

12. How does a **satellite** get into space?

_____

13. Where would you like to go on a space **flight**?

_____

14. What things in nature do you **observe**?

_____

15. When do astronauts take **spacewalks**?

_____

Academic Words

D. Read each sentence. Write a new sentence using the underlined word.

16. Learning to swim can be a <u>challenge</u>.

_____

17. The girls <u>achieve</u> their goal when they swim across the pool.

_____

Write the key words. Tell a family member what they mean.

116

Name _____ Date _____

Reader's Companion

Use with Student Book pages 226–233.

Franklin's Dream

In 1980, Franklin was chosen to become an astronaut. He started to train in classrooms and in labs. After six years of training, he was ready. Franklin first flew with *Columbia* in 1986.

Franklin would go on six more space flights. As an astronaut, he did experiments. He made spacewalks and repaired things. Franklin went on more space flights than anyone had ever gone on before.

Flying in space is exciting. But for Franklin, the sight of Earth from outer space is the best part. He says that it is very beautiful. He says that we must take care of Earth.

"Earth is humanity's spaceship and the only one we have," says Franklin. "We must protect it."

Use What You Know

List two things you would like to do in the future.

1. _____

2. _____

Reading Strategy

Circle three important details that you would include in a summary.

Comprehension Check

What does Franklin say is the best part of being an astronaut? Underline the answer.

Use the Strategy

Summarize the first two paragraphs of the passage.

_____

_____

_____

Retell It!

Retell the last two paragraphs of the passage. Pretend you are Franklin Chang-Diaz talking to a group of children.

_____

_____

_____

_____

_____

Reader's Response

Why do you think the story of Franklin Chang-Diaz is important?

_____

_____

_____

Home-School Connection Retell the passage to a family member.

Name _____ Date _____

Phonics: *R-Controlled Vowels ar, or, ore*

Use with Student Book page 234.

> **The letter *r* changes vowel sounds.**

**Read each sentence. Underline the words with the letters *ar*.
Circle the words with the letters *or* or *ore*.**

1. Can you throw the ball far?

2. I sat on my porch and read the story.

3. Some sports are hard to play.

4. My dog started to bark.

5. The marching band performed at the state fair.

6. Eight planets orbit the sun.

7. I scored a point before you got to the game.

8. The store window was dark.

9. Every morning, I feed the horses in the barn.

10. The drivers in the cars honked their horns!

 **Think of two words each that have the sounds *ar* and *or/ore*.
Share the words with a family member.**

Comprehension: Summarize

Use with Student Book pages 236–237.

Read the passage. Then write a summary of the passage.

Mars

Mars is the fourth planet from our sun. Scientists sent a robot to Mars. The robot helps us learn about this planet.

There is ice on Mars. Scientists do not know if there are any living things. Some scientists think that there may be tiny living things under the planet's surface. Others think there may be some living things under the ice.

_____

_____

_____

_____

Home-School Connection Summarize an episode of a TV show for a family member.

Name _____ Date _____

Grammar: Past Tense Verbs

Use with Student Book page 238.

> **Past tense verbs** name actions that already happened.

A. Read the sentences. Put a check by each sentence that tells about something that already happened.

1. _____ We moved to a different city.

2. _____ Mom and Dad walk in the park every evening.

3. _____ We carried our chairs down to the beach.

4. _____ I will do my homework after dinner.

B. Complete each sentence. Use the past tense form of the verb.

5. I _____ a cake for my brother's birthday.
    (bake)

6. The young girl _____ home after school.
    (hurry)

7. Last night, my best friend _____ me on the phone.
    (call)

8. We _____ up after the party.
    (clean)

Write sentences using the past tense of the verbs *look*, *paint*, and *dry*. Share your sentences with a family member.

121

Spelling: Long *i* Spelled *igh*

Use with Student Book page 239.

bright	lightning	night
right	sight	

SPELLING TIP

The /ī/ sound can be spelled with the letters *igh*.

Read each clue. Write the word that matches the clue.

1. one of the five senses _____

2. happens during a storm _____

3. shining strongly _____

4. opposite of day _____

5. correct _____

Write a story using three words with *igh*.

_____

_____

_____

_____

Home-School Connection With a family member, write a poem using words that rhyme with *night*.

Name _____   Date _____

Vocabulary
Use with Student Book pages 240–241.

Key Words

bark

rainbow

canoe

handprints

A. Choose the word that *best* completes each sentence. Write the word.

1. They crossed the lake in a wooden

   _____.

2. After the storm, we saw a beautiful _____ in the sky.

3. I used dried leaves and tree _____ to make a fire.

4. We left our _____ in the wet sand.

B. Read each clue. Circle the key word in the row of letters.

5. outer part of a tree trunk

   c a p o e s b a r k b o w s i n t s

6. marks made by pressing your hands onto something soft

   r o w e h a n d p r i n t s d s b k

7. rounded row of colors seen in the sky

   p r e d r a i n b o w c o e b w s t

8. narrow wooden boat with pointed end

   p o e r s t l b o e h d s c a n o e

123

C. Answer the questions.

9. Who might use a **canoe**?

_____

10. What colors have you seen in a **rainbow**?

_____

11. Where have you left your **handprints**?

_____

12. Why is **bark** important?

_____

Academic Words

D. Read each sentence. Write a new sentence using the underlined word.

13. Write a summary of the passage.

_____

14. Let's link arms and walk together.

_____

Home-School Connection With a family member, write a story using the key words.

124

Name _____ Date _____

Reader's Companion

Use with Student Book pages 242–245.

One Moon, Many Myths

A myth from India tells about the sun and the moon.

Earth Mother had two children. She loved them very much. She wanted them to live forever. So she sent her children into the sky. Her son became the sun. Her daughter became the moon.

The daughter rose into the sky. Earth Mother wanted to hug her one last time. But it was too late. She could only touch her daughter's cheek. Earth Mother left her handprints on the moon.

Use What You Know

Name one thing you see on the moon.

_____

_____

Reading Strategy

MARK the TEXT

Compare the son and the daughter. Underline three ways they are alike.

Genre

MARK the TEXT

What part of nature does this myth explain? Circle the answer.

125

Use the Strategy

Contrast the son and the daughter. Tell how they are different.

_____

_____

Retell It!

Retell the passage as if you were the son or daughter.

_____

_____

_____

_____

Reader's Response

What thing in nature do you wonder about? Tell what you would make up a myth about.

_____

_____

_____

Home-School Connection Retell the passage to a family member.

Name _____ Date _____

Word Analysis: Multiple-Meaning Words

Use with Student Book page 246.

> **Multiple-meaning words** have more than one meaning.

Read each sentence. Look at the word in bold type. Then circle the *best* meaning for the word.

1. I hurt my **calf** when I ran the race.

> young cow
>
> soft back part of a leg

2. My **palm** hurt after I caught the ball.

> tree with large, pointed leaves
>
> inside surface of the hand

3. The **sound** was loud and scary.

> something you hear
>
> healthy and strong

4. I ate an **ear** of corn at dinner.

> part of the body that you hear with
>
> part of some plants where the grains grow

With a family member, write sentences for the other meanings of the words.

Comprehension: Compare and Contrast

Use with Student Book pages 248–249.

Read the passage. Answer the questions.

Venus and Mars

Venus is about the same size as Earth. It is the second planet from the sun. Venus has thick clouds all around it. This planet is very hot, and it does not have water. Venus has mountains, volcanoes, and craters.

Mars is smaller than Earth. It is the fourth planet from the sun. Mars is usually cold. This planet has ice. Mars has mountains, volcanoes, and craters.

1. Compare Venus and Mars. List two ways they are similar.

_____

_____

2. Contrast Venus and Mars. List two ways they are different.

_____

_____

Summarize the passage for a family member.

Name _____ Date _____

Grammar: Future Tense Verbs

Use with Student Book page 250.

> Use the helping word *will* to form a **future tense verb**.

A. **Underline the sentences that tell about an action that is going to happen in the future.**

1. I will eat everything on my plate.

2. He went to the mall with friends.

3. My brother will swim the fastest.

4. We helped paint the house.

5. Those trees will bloom in spring.

B. **Complete each sentence. Use the future tense form of the verb.**

6. My parents (drive) _____ us to the beach.

7. School (close) _____ early today.

8. Our plane (land) _____ at noon.

9. You (like) _____ what I got for you!

10. The storm (begin) _____ tomorrow morning.

 With a family member, write four sentences using the future tense form of *laugh, dream, jump,* and *make.*

129

Spelling: *Two, Too,* and *To*

Use with Student Book page 251.

Write *two, too,* or *to* to complete each sentence.

SPELLING TIP

Here are some tips to spell *two, too,* and *to*.
Two = 2
Too has too many o's!
To is spelled like *go*. I will *go to* the store.

1. I will bring my games

   _____ your house.

2. You need more than

   _____ players!

3. _____ of my friends are coming.

4. I'll teach them, _____ .

5. Can I play, _____ ?

 Write a story using *two, too,* and *to*.

_____

_____

_____

Home-School Connection Explain the meanings of *two, too,* and *to* to a family member.

Name _____ Date _____

Review

Use with Student Book pages 204–251.

Answer the questions after reading Unit 5. You can go back and reread to help find the answers.

1. Review *Earth and Beyond*. What is on the surface of the moon? Circle the letter of the correct answer.

   a. dust, gas, plants, animals
   b. dust, mountains, craters
   c. gas, asteroids, mountains
   d. craters, meteors, animals

2. Review the passage about the stars. Then write what you learned about constellations.

   _____

   _____

3. Read these sentences.

   Earth is a sphere. It is a large, round ball in space.

   What does *sphere* mean? Circle the letter of the correct answer.

   a. something large
   b. something in space
   c. something round
   d. a kind of game

4. Review *Franklin's Dream*. Write a summary about what he did as a child. Include three important details.

_____

_____

_____

5. Why do you think Franklin was able to make spacewalks to repair things on the space shuttle?

_____

_____

_____

6. In *One Moon, Many Myths,* how did Hina get to the moon? Circle the letter of the correct answer.

a. She took a canoe.   **c.** She rose into the sky.

b. She climbed a rainbow.   **d.** Her son became the sun.

7. Compare what you learned about the moon in the myth *Baloo the Moon* and the selection *Earth and Beyond*.

_____

_____

_____

Home-School Connection Tell a family member something new you learned from this unit.

Name _____ Date _____

Vocabulary
Use with Student Book pages 262–263.

Key Words

festival

annual

advertise

schedule

supplies

A. **Choose the word that *best* completes each sentence. Write the word.**

1. Was there music and dancing

at the _____ ?

2. We need to buy pencils and other _____ for school.

3. We made a poster to _____ our play.

4. The spring party is an _____ event. It takes place on May 1 each year.

5. The _____ tells us what time the movie begins.

B. **Read each clue. Write the word that matches the clue.**

6. list of events and times   _____

7. happening once a year   _____

8. big event   _____

9. announce an event   _____

10. things you need for school   _____

C. Answer the questions.

11. What might you see at an arts **festival**?

_____

12. Where do people **advertise**?

_____

13. How is a **schedule** helpful?

_____

14. What is your favorite **annual** event?

_____

15. What **supplies** do firefighters need?

_____

Academic Words

D. Read each sentence. Write a new sentence using the underlined word.

16. The teacher will <u>illustrate</u> how to use verbs in a sentence.

_____

17. Pencils and paper are <u>available</u> at the store.

_____

 Use each key word in a sentence. Share your sentences with a family member.

Name _____ Date _____

Reader's Companion

Use with Student Book pages 264–267.

Arts Festival!

The town of Red Tree has an arts festival each year. It is called the Summer Arts Festival. All the people in the town come.

Children and adults can take art classes. They can go to a demonstration to learn how to make pottery or a collage.

Use What You Know

List two kinds of art you like to make.

1. _____

2. _____

Reading Strategy

MARK the TEXT

What does the author tell about? Circle the answer.

Comprehension Check

MARK the TEXT

Underline two things people can do at the Summer Arts Festival.

135

Use the Strategy

What is the author's purpose in writing this passage?

_____

_____

_____

Retell It!

Retell the passage. Pretend you are trying to get people to come to the Summer Arts Festival.

_____

_____

_____

_____

Reader's Response

What would you like to do at the arts festival? Why?

_____

_____

_____

Name _____ Date _____

Phonics: Diphthongs *ou* and *ow*

Use with Student Book page 268.

> The diphthongs *ou* and *ow* have
> the sound you hear in *house*.

**Read each sentence. Underline the words with the diphthongs
ou and *ow*.**

1. The apple fell down onto the ground.

2. Cows and owls are animals.

3. Dad shouted "Wow!" when he saw a mouse.

4. Every scout wore a brown cap.

5. Why is the clown frowning?

6. I followed the crowd outside.

7. All of the clouds were round and puffy.

8. Kara found a dime under the couch.

9. We heard a loud sound!

10. We drove south to get to town.

 **Make a list of the *ou* words. Make a list of the *ow* words. Read
the words on your lists to a family member.**

Comprehension: Author's Purpose

Use with Student Book pages 270–271.

Read the passage. Then answer the questions.

The Art Show

Dear Grandmother,

Please come to the Woodland Art Show. It will be at Woodland Elementary School on Saturday.

My artwork will be in the show. I have a painting of your cat, Tiger. I have a photograph of a tree, too.

Please come see my painting and photograph.

Love,

Julio

1. What is the author's purpose?

_____

2. Give two details that explain the author's purpose.

_____

_____

 Retell the passage to a family member. Explain what the author's purpose is.

Name _____ Date _____

Grammar: Commas in a Series

Use with Student Book page 272.

> **You can list things in a sentence.**
> **Put commas after each item in the list.**

Look for lists in the sentences. Add commas.

1. I have band practice on Thursday Friday and Saturday.

2. We made a donation of clothing food and blankets.

3. The students danced sang and played games.

4. Every summer fall and winter I play on a sports team.

5. I left my art supplies school books and eyeglasses at home.

6. June July and August are my favorite months.

7. We saw elephants zebras and lions at the zoo.

8. His hair eyes and shirt were all brown.

9. I brought my little sister my best friend and my dog to the park.

10. Julia Marisol and Tina are on my team.

 **Write a sentence. Tell about three things you like. Be sure to put commas in your list. Share your sentence with a family member.**

Spelling: Words with *sch*
Use with Student Book page 273.

schedule	scheme	scholar
school	schooner	

SPELLING TIP

In some words, *sch* spells the sound /sk/.

Read each clue. Write the word that matches the clue.

1. place where children learn _____

2. type of boat _____

3. secret plan _____

4. list of when events take place _____

5. someone who knows about a subject _____

 Fill in the chart to show your schedule in school.

Time	Activity

Home-School Connection   Write a sentence using each word. Read your sentences to a family member.

Name _____ Date _____

Vocabulary
Use with Student Book pages 274–275.

Use with Student Book pages 274–275.

A. Choose the word that *best* completes each sentence. Write the word.

Key Words
puppets
scissors
stapler
yarn
buttons

1. Do not run when you are

carrying _____.

2. I need a _____ to put
these sheets of paper together.

3. I help my brother with the _____
on his coat.

4. My mom helped me knit with _____.

5. In art class, we made _____ that fit on
our fingers.

**B. Read each clue. Find the key word in the row of letters.
Then circle the word.**

6. toys that fit over your hand
and can be moved

t d a p u p p e t s o b

7. used to make sweaters

y e p p s i c a y a r n

8. used to cut paper

p s c i s s o r s l r n

9. used to keep pieces of
paper together

d e r a s t a p l e r t

10. used to close shirts and coats

b u t t o n s e d p s

C. Answer the questions.

11. How can you make **puppets** move?

_____

12. What do you use **scissors** for?

_____

13. What would you use a **stapler** for?

_____

14. What are some things that are made with **yarn**?

_____

15. Where can you find **buttons**?

_____

Academic Words

D. Read each sentence. Write a new sentence using the underlined word.

16. Families <u>contribute</u> used computers to help the Kids' Club.

_____

17. My <u>design</u> shows where the tables and chairs will go in the room.

_____

 Use the key words to write about an art project you would like to do. Share your writing with a family member.

Name _____ Date _____

Reader's Companion

Use with Student Book pages 276–281.

How to Make Puppets

What You Will Need

white paper plates

scissors

stapler

glue

yarn

buttons

colored paper

crayons, markers, or paint

MARK the TEXT

Use the Strategy

What is your purpose for reading this passage?

_____

_____

_____

Retell It!

Retell this passage as if you were showing a friend how to make a puppet.

_____

_____

_____

_____

Reader's Response

What would you have a puppet say and do?

_____

_____

_____

Summarize the passage for a family member.

Name _____ Date _____

Word Analysis: Use a Dictionary

Use with Student Book page 282.

> You can look up words in a **dictionary** to find out what they mean. Some words have more than one meaning.

Read each sentence. Look at the underlined word. Then circle the letter of the *best* meaning for the word.

1. Children like to <u>play</u> with puppets.

   a. performance on a stage
   b. have fun with

2. The rocket zoomed up into <u>space</u>.

   a. area past Earth
   b. place where you can put something

3. I read a <u>lot</u> of books last summer.

   a. area of land
   b. large number

4. A whale has a very big <u>mouth</u>.

   a. place where a river enters the ocean
   b. body part used for speaking and eating

Look up the word *right* in a dictionary. Write two sentences using two different meanings of the word. Share your sentences with a family member.

Comprehension: Purpose for Reading

Use with Student Book pages 284–285.

Put a check by your purpose for reading.

1. Why would you read a cake recipe?

_____ to enjoy

_____ to learn new facts or ideas

_____ to learn how to do something

2. Why would you read an article about animals in South America?

_____ to enjoy

_____ to learn new facts or ideas

_____ to learn how to do something

3. Why would you read a mystery story?

_____ to enjoy

_____ to learn new facts or ideas

_____ to learn how to do something

4. Why would you read a billboard about a new movie?

_____ to enjoy

_____ to learn new facts or ideas

_____ to learn how to do something

 **With a family member, read the weather report in the newspaper. Tell what the purpose for reading it is.**

Name _____ Date _____

Grammar: Directive Sentences

Use with Student Book page 286.

> **Directive sentences** tell the reader to do something.

A. Read the sentences. Put a check by the directive sentences.

1. _____ Write your name on top of the page.

2. _____ Draw a picture of your family.

3. _____ How many people are in your family?

4. _____ Show what your family likes to do.

5. _____ Making art is fun!

B. Use the word to write a directive sentence. The first one is done for you.

6. Look <u>both ways before you cross the street.</u>

7. Close _____

8. Put _____

9. Listen _____

10. Give _____

Home-School Connection With a family member, write the directions for playing a favorite game. Include at least three directive sentences.

147

Spelling: The /j/ Sound

Use with Student Book page 287.

Read each sentence. Unscramble the underlined letters to complete the missing word.

1. Diamonds, rubies, and emeralds are <u>mse</u>.

   g ____ ____ ____

2. Will you perform <u>aimc</u> tricks in the show?

   ____ ____ g ____ ____

3. A <u>frafei</u> has a long neck.

   g ____ ____ ____ ____ ____

4. Be <u>telne</u> with the little kitten.

   g ____ ____ ____ ____

5. There can be <u>stain</u> in fairy tales.

   g ____ ____ ____ ____

Write a story. Use four of the words with *g*.

_____

_____

_____

 **Home-School Connection** With a family member, list four more words that have the /j/ sound spelled with a *g*.

Name _____ Date _____

Vocabulary

Use with Student Book pages 288–289.

A. Choose the word that *best* completes each sentence. Write the word.

Key Words

microphone

guitar

trumpet

performer

soles

rhythm

1. Hot sand can burn the

    _____ of your feet!

2. A _____ has strings.

3. Blow into the _____ to play a note.

4. Clap your hands to follow the _____!

5. The speaker used a _____ so everyone
    could hear him.

6. That drummer is a good _____ .

B. Write TRUE or FALSE.

7. Rhythm is the pattern of beats in music.   _____

8. A microphone will make a sound softer.   _____

9. A trumpet is played in a high school band. _____

10. Soles are the top part of the foot.   _____

C. **Answer the questions.**

11. How does someone play a **guitar**?

_____

12. Why do different shoes have different kinds of **soles**?

_____

13. How can someone keep a **rhythm**?

_____

14. How does someone play a **trumpet**?

_____

15. Why would a **performer** use a **microphone**?

_____

Academic Words

D. **Read each sentence. Write a new sentence using the underlined word.**

16. The <u>source</u> of the stream is a lake in the mountains.

_____

17. <u>Select</u> three books to check out of the library.

_____

 **Write a riddle for each of the key words. For example, "You walk on me, but I'm not the ground. What am I?" Your *soles*!**

Name _____ Date _____

Reader's Companion

Use with Student Book pages 290–293.

The Music Goes On

Last week, people who love music went to River City Park. The River City Music Festival had special sounds and sights. People heard great music. They saw beautiful dancers.

This year, the festival had an international theme. The music and dance came from many different countries.

Use What You Know

Name your favorite song.

_____

_____

Reading Strategy

MARK the TEXT

Underline a clue that helps you to conclude that different types of music were played in the festival.

Comprehension Check

Where was the festival held? Circle the answer.

MARK the TEXT

Use the Strategy

Do you think you would have liked the music festival? Tell why.

_____

_____

_____

Retell It!

Retell this passage as if you were speaking on a radio program.

_____

_____

_____

_____

Reader's Response

What is your favorite type of music? What do you like most about that music?

_____

_____

_____

Home-School Connection   **Summarize the passage for a family member.**

Name _____ Date _____

Word Analysis: Multi-Syllable Words

Use with Student Book page 294.

> In a **multi-syllable word,** each syllable
> has one vowel sound.

Read each word. Count the syllables and write the word in the correct column.

| complicated | dictionary | festival | microphone | music |
| popular | quartet | traditional | trumpet | |

Two Syllables	_____
	_____
	_____
Three Syllables	_____
	_____
	_____
Four Syllables	_____
	_____
	_____

Read the words in each column to a family member.

Comprehension: Draw a Conclusion

Use with Student Book pages 296–297.

Read the passage. Then answer the questions.

Patricia's Letter

Dear Diego,

   The music contest is finally over. I played my favorite song on the guitar. I was really scared. My parents were sitting in the front row. I knew I did well from the way people clapped. I couldn't believe it when they called my name. I rushed onto the stage. My ribbon is blue and gold. I even got my picture in the newspaper.

Love, Patricia

1. What do you know about contests?

_____

2. Underline three details that happened to Patricia.

3. Think about what you know and read. Now draw a conclusion. What happened to Patricia at the music contest?

_____

Retell the passage to a family member.

Name _____ Date _____

Grammar: Direct Quotation

Use with Student Book page 298.

> A **direct quotation** tells the exact words a person said.

A. Read each sentence. Circle the name of the person who is talking. Underline the words being said.

1. Laurie said, "I love to play guitar!"

2. "Do you need help?" Tilly asked.

3. "I think playing the trumpet is hard," Mary declared.

4. Ronaldo said, "We don't have a microphone."

B. Read each sentence. Add quotation marks to show the direct quotations.

5. This is my first concert, Jonah said.

6. The judge said, You are the winner!

7. I was so surprised, Patricia told us.

8. Bud asked, May I borrow your drumsticks?

 Write five direct quotations based on something you hear friends or family members say. Share your sentences with a family member.

Spelling: Spell Check

Use with Student Book page 299.

Read the sentences. Correctly spell the underlined words.

1. Can you hand me the <u>sciscors</u>, please?

    _____

2. I need a <u>microfone</u> to sing. _____

3. These flowers are <u>beautyfull</u>. _____

4. Margarita is a great <u>danser</u>. _____

5. This was the best <u>consert</u> I have ever been to!

    _____

 **List five words you have trouble spelling. Make sure you spell each word correctly.**

_____

_____

_____

_____

_____

Home-School Connection Ask a family member to say these words out loud: *guitar, trumpet, festival, contribute, music.* Try to spell the words.

Name _____ Date _____

Review

Use with Student Book pages 256–299.

Answer the questions after reading Unit 6. You can go back and reread to help find the answers.

1. In *Arts Festival!*, what is the contest at the Summer Arts Festival in Red Tree? Circle the letter of the correct answer.

   a. Poster-Making Contest
   b. Letter-Writing Contest
   c. Pottery-Making Contest
   d. Puppet-Making Contest

2. Look at the poster on page 265. What is the author's purpose in making this poster? Circle the letter of the correct answer.

   a. entertain
   b. direct
   c. persuade
   d. enjoy

3. Read these sentences from the selection.

   > The town of Red Tree has an arts festival each year. This annual event is called the Summer Arts Festival.

   What does *annual* mean?

   _____

   _____

4. What is your purpose for reading *How to Make Puppets*? Circle the letter of the correct answer.

    a. to gather paper plates and yarn
    b. to learn how to make a puppet
    c. to learn how to knit a sweater
    d. to learn the history of puppets

5. Look at the sock puppet on page 280. What could you add to this puppet?

_____

_____

_____

6. *The Music Goes On* states that young people are an important part of the festival. List three details that show this is true.

_____

_____

_____

7. Why do you think Shakira Gopal may be a good dancer? List two reasons.

_____

_____

_____

 **Home-School Connection**   Tell a family member something new you learned in this unit.